The Al Fresco Life

POOLS, SPAS, BARS, AND KITCHENS

Schiffer
Publishing Ltd

4880 Lower Valley Road, Atglen, Pennsylvania 19310

**Joe Vassallo
and Mary Vail**

Dedication

Proceeds from the sale of this publication will go to the Nevada Clark County School District Title-1 HOPE, Homeless Education Program to assist disadvantaged and homeless students with essential school supplies and other basic needs.

A curious hummingbird is caught in mid-flight during this time-exposure image.

Designed by Mark David Bowyer
Type set in NewsGoth Cn BT / Dutch809 BT

ISBN: 978-0-7643-3188-6
Printed in China

Schiffer Books are available at special discounts for bulk purchases for sales promotions or premiums. Special editions, including personalized covers, corporate imprints, and excerpts can be created in large quantities for special needs. For more information contact the publisher:

Published by Schiffer Publishing Ltd.
4880 Lower Valley Road
Atglen, PA 19310
Phone: (610) 593-1777; Fax: (610) 593-2002
E-mail: Info@schifferbooks.com

For the largest selection of fine reference books on this and related subjects, please visit our web site at
www.schifferbooks.com
We are always looking for people to write books on new and related subjects. If you have an idea for a book please contact us at the above address.

This book may be purchased from the publisher.
Include $5.00 for shipping.
Please try your bookstore first.
You may write for a free catalog.

In Europe, Schiffer books are distributed by
Bushwood Books
6 Marksbury Ave.
Kew Gardens
Surrey TW9 4JF England
Phone: 44 (0) 20 8392-8585; Fax: 44 (0) 20 8392-9876
E-mail: info@bushwoodbooks.co.uk
Website: www.bushwoodbooks.co.uk
Free postage in the U.K., Europe; air mail at cost.

Contents

Acknowledgments

This book would not have been possible without Paragon Pools' incredible personnel; the talented designer team of Joseph Anthony Vassallo, CBP; Hank Wiesenthal, and Bill Sachanko; the administrative staff of Trish Johnson, Damon McBride, Ashley Vail and Sean Vail, and the construction department of John Stanton, John Tomasello and Mary Jean Paradis. Their visions and building expertise has resulted in Las Vegas' most desired backyard retreats.

Much gratitude to the manufacturers and subcontractors, their devotion to delivering exceptional products and services allow us to bring the design to fruition.

To the architects, interior designers, custom builders, homebuilders, landscape designers and homeowners who sought out Paragon Pools for their design and construction projects, thank you for trusting we would meet and exceed your expectations.

Appreciation to the pool owners whom granted us access into their private sanctuaries, allowing us to capture these breathtaking images.

To Certified Master Chef Gustav Mauler and Executive Chef Emilio LaScala of Spiedini Ristorante, thank you for the tempting food styling.

Thanks to my wife, Alana Vassallo who assisted on many of the photography shoots.

And lastly but not least, thanks to my co-author, Mary Vail, for her perseverance, dedication, and inspiration.

—Joe Vassallo

Introduction

This book showcases some of the most desired *al fresco* retreats in Las Vegas. The pools and spas were constructed by Paragon Pools, most as original custom designs by Vassallo and his design team and others as collaborations between Paragon Pools and the homeowners, architects and homebuilders. Some of the elements that complete the backyard habitats, such as landscaping and adjacent structures, were provided by additional industry professionals.

Vassallo introduces several new concepts to enhance your knowledge of pool design. He encourages you to abandon the stereotypical idea of a pool and spa, allowing your imagination to say "why not." As you peruse the pages, you will learn about *Aquatekture™*, how to develop a *Comfort-scape™*, when to incorporate special treatments such as an infinity edge, *Wet-Flame™* or a *Liquid-Window™*, the excite-ment of taking a *Virtual Water Tour™*, determining if a *Pixie Pool™* is perfect for you, and of course how to enjoy the ultimate *al fresco* lifestyle.

Often a single image was not enough to capture the full beauty of the pool and spa. Therefore, whenever possible, a variety of angles provides diverse views for full appreciation of the setting.

Fellow Las Vegans Certified Master Chef Gustav Mauler (Grilling chapter with recipes) and Mixologist Shawn Barker (Poolside Potions chapter with drinks) join Vassallo and Vail in providing expertise on entertaining and getting the most out of one's culinary corner.

And finally, what makes each pool a special place for the homeowner is the personal touch of adornments, furnishings, and accessories that owners incorporate into their outdoor surroundings.

Living The Al Fresco Lifestyle!

Al Fresco, Italian for "in the fresh air," is typically associated with dining outdoors at fancy restaurants, European bistros, or sidewalk cantinas. But for those who truly indulge in being outdoors, living the *al fresco* lifestyle is a way of life.

More and more homeowners are looking to create complete open-air additions of their homes — requesting specific areas for cooking, bar service, lounging and high-tech entertainment vignettes around their pool.

The exterior of the home is valuable real estate, however most homeowners underutilize the full potential of the land surrounding the house. Increase the usable living space by minimizing the turf and softscape, incorporating greenery as accents much like one does inside the home with pottery or in isolated planters. You can carve out a craft corner, an alcove to enjoy your morning coffee, a meditation area or a place to host the family meal every night.

Your *al fresco* setting is an extension of the interior design; with televisions, stereo systems, fireplaces and culinary space. An abundance of weather friendly products such as outdoor lighting, fans, rugs and heaters provide almost year-round use in any climate. Stylish furnishings with high durable, easy to clean and quick dry fabrics give you an unlimited supply of style options.

Don't be afraid to cover the property line walls with exterior tile, stone or paints, this will give the walls a finished look, and going vertical with decking materials has become very trendy.

Palapas, cabanas, patio covers and drapery help to identify specific *al fresco* spaces as well as enhance the intimacy of the setting. Resorts and hotels are capitalizing on the concept, converting large open outdoor areas into secluded sanctuaries throughout the property for private dining, spa treatments and lounging areas.

Succumb to the *al fresco* lifestyle to enhance your mental and physical well-being.

Break the boundaries of the backyard and create something illuminating, exciting and memorable, even mystifying.

An enclosed spa and multi-tier pool with a linear fire element, dual WetFlames and a Liquid-Window provides for year-round al fresco living.

Aquatekture™

You may have seen the commercial where the affluent couple meets with a talented architect. Placing a faucet on the desk, the couple asks him to build a house around the faucet.

That is exactly how I see a pool with regards to the surrounding exterior space. As a pool designer and builder, it is the aqueous elements that are the centerpiece, the focal point, with all the other architectural facets as complimentary components.

This is what I identify as Aquatekture™, the discipline of designing, engineering and erecting water environments and ancillary components in a harmonious nature with consideration to function, space and aesthetics.

For centuries, water has played a significant influence in architectural design. Most notably Roman baths, Egyptian aqueducts, and of course the city built on water, Venice, Italy.

More recently, trendy designers and architects have been influenced by the ancient Chinese practice of Fung shui, incorporating the five basic natural elements of water, wood, fire, earth, and metal to achieve better health, wealth and harmony in one's life.

This backyard is a perfect example of Aquatekture, a small, basic rectangular pool with adjoining spa is transformed into something spectacular.

Successful Aquatekture™ does not require a six-digit budget or every accessory available on the market. A giant waterfall, lavish planting, custom furnishings, imported tile and sunken barbeques do not guarantee great Aquatekture™.

Good design may happen by accident, but great Aquatekture™ is the result of a trained, talented and focused designer who time and again creates extraordinary spaces to fulfill the client's desires within a specified budget.

Another perfect example of Aquatekture, a small, basic rectangular pool with adjoining spa.

Creating a Comfort-scape™

We are all familiar with comfort foods. As my good friend, Certified Master Chef Gustav Mauler, notes, "Comfort foods are cuisine that gives us joy, warmth, and familiarity with our past. People look to comfort foods for many reasons; to calm them and relieve stress during sad times, to celebrate a special event or achievement, or to reward themselves for something well-done."

The same sense of solace can be achieved through scenery in a backyard and pool design, which I call a Comfort-scape™.

Comfort-scape™ is achieving a sense of joy, a feeling of warmth or an awakening of fond memories through scenery in the pool and yard design by blending all elements of the environment from planting and ground materials, to color schemes, fabrics, furnishings and accessories.

It may not be possible to pack up one's family and move to their favorite vacation spot, such as the Caribbean, but recreating it is possible. Thanks to the influx of design tools, outdoor friendly furnishings and appliances readily accessible, homeowners can easily create their own personal Comfort-scape™. Durable composite woods of cedar, teak and eucalyptus as well as weather resistant outdoor fabrics and flooring surfaces of travertine, limestone and ceramic tiles make it almost effortless to achieve one's objective.

For the ranch lover, horses and cattle may not be an option depending on where one resides, but the use of rustic wood furnishings, leather, cowboy inspired accents and log fences will certainly create the country Comfort-scape™ one is trying to capture.

The serene environment of a spa Comfort-scape™ might be composed of Buddha statues, a selection of bamboo planting, reed mats, soft hues of natural tones, pagoda ornaments and a meditation area with a trickling pond.

A nautical theme with red, white and blue creates an east coast Comfort-scape™. Buoys, oars, a lighthouse, a boat's wheel, anchors, ropes with nautical knots, and signal flags complete the setting.

Even with the simplest of pools, one's Comfort-scape™ can be achieved with the right accessories.

The homeowner duplicated a Las Cabos, Mexico, experience for their Comfort-scape. The excitement of Cabo was captured with satillo tile accents in the pool and patio area and the use of vibrant primary colors of red, orange, yellow and blue highlight walls, pillows, umbrellas and other furnishings. Mexican honeysuckle, bird of paradise, and queen palms surround the yard and Mexican architecture shapes the outdoor kitchen.

Virtual Water Tour™

One of the most challenging aspects a homeowner is faced with in finalizing a pool design is actually visualizing how the pool will look and function in relation to the home and yard.

Working with thousands of pool buyers over the years, I came to understand that very few people could actually visualize from an architectural plan view. Most could not grasp what the completed project would look like from the detailed technical drawings.

Some designers use a two-dimensional color rendering to assist homeowners. And even with different colors designating separate aspects of the design; blue for the pool, green for the landscaping and brown tones for the decking; the elevations, depths, and isometric details are still missing.

Several years ago, a computer wiz-kid named Noah Nehlich approached me with the concept of taking the pool plan and computerizing it into a three-dimensional, animated design program presentation.

Incorporating the same software imaging used to create the uncanny realism of popular video games, Noah's program gives homeowners a limitless view

Structure Studios 3-D program allows the pool designer to transport homeowners through a Virtual Water Tour; in, around and above the pool. Shown, 3-D view of the pool from the walking mode.

from every angle of the yard: above, behind, through the interior of the home and submerged underwater, in what I call the Virtual Water Tour™.

We introduced the 3-D program to the public in 2001 at a luxury home tour in Las Vegas. Noah showcased his presentation on my WetFlame™ pool and home, designed by Architect Richard Luke. The reviews were as we expected; people were fascinated with the results.

Using this software, trained designers take the house and lot plan, insert the windows, sliding doors, back walls, siding, and drop the custom pool design into the yard. From there, the designer has thousands of landscaping items and finishing materials to choose from, including decking, interior pool finish, outdoor kitchens, patios, palapas, fire pits, waterfalls, tile, rockwork, slides, diving boards, lighting and the list goes on. The program is extremely helpful in optimizing space when developing the aquatekture, creating a Comfort-scape™, or designing a Pixie pool™ for a small backyard.

Noah's company, Structure Studios, now spans the globe with thousands of pool builders actively using the program in fifteen countries including the US, Europe, Australia, Mexico, and the United Arab Emirates.

Turn on the waterfall, heat up the spa, light the fire pit, let the kids go down the slide to enjoy the pool even before the first scoop of dirt is lifted!

Actual photograph from same point of view at dusk.

Photograph from same point at mid-day.

Classic Chic

Timeless designs of Grecian, rectangle, kidney, freeform, and oval are blended with modern materials

Off-set rectangles put neatly into place give this backyard a crisp look.

This classic Grecian designed pool is accented with coastal materials; cedar wood walls, fishnets and glass balls.

The linear shape of these pools are complimented by the walls and decks.

This traditional rectangle pool features a large wet deck for lounging.

Raised, planters, fountain bubblers and water features create a backdrop for this pool.

**Freeform pools create an inviting
setting in these backyards.**

The large putting green adds additional activity for pool goers.

Separating the pool and fountain are strips of grass that divide the deck into squares, giving this pool a chic look.

Classic Grecian designs can be
modified to take on different looks.

The tumbled paver decking gives this pool an old world ambiance.

Classic Chic

This Italian themed backyard celebrates the homeowner's ancestry.

Corner set spas accent these rectangular shaped pools.

The large covered patio and grand wet deck provide a cozy conversation area.

A large circular wet deck extends into the classic Grecian pool.

Serpentine walls gives these pools a unique freeform look.

The raised spa and decking are finished with natural stone.

Stamped concrete, natural stone wet deck and fire pit combined with
a ledger stone spa work together to give this backyard a great look.

Nature Inspired

Designs that incorporate native materials, colors, textures and shapes inherent to the environment

Large natural boulders and ledger stone highlight this multi-level pool.

Sculptured stone waterfalls create
the backdrop for this pool.

The large platform lounge deck adds elevation to the pool setting.

A variety of interior finishes give each of these pools a distinctive look.

A combination of real and sculptured stone give this pool a tropical look.

A swim-up grotto provides a cozy nook.

Red sandstone native to the area defines this pool.

A stoned wall with sheer descent water features is the focal point of this unique shaped pool.

The Tuscan look of this pool setting was achieved by using ledger stone, gauze drapery and grapevines.

A sprinkling of boulders adds a natural look to the pool.

Waterfalls and ledger stone are popular features in nature inspired pools.

A multi-leveled stream spills into the pool.

Hurricane palms, rock boulders, pebble interior and a thatched hut allowed this homeowner to achieve his Hawaiian Comfort-scape.

Succulent landscaping line this desert oasis.

Variations in rockwork gives these pools unique natural looks.

Sculptured stone outline the pool, oversized grotto, waterfalls and adjoining sunken kitchen.

A combination waterfall and slide is created from natural and sculpted stone.

This Japanese comfort-scape was created through the use of oriental accents, bamboo, torches and polished black pebbles.

Casual Contemporary

The softening of traditional shapes and formal
structures with warm earthy tones, natural
materials, and wispy landscapes for a touch of avant-garde

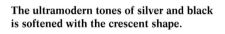

The ultramodern tones of silver and black is softened with the crescent shape.

Water flows continuously into this pool from four strategic points; the water wall, the reflection pond, the spa and the diving platforms.

Field stone cabanas and fountain simulate a northern Italian villa.

Multiple settee areas provide for a variety of gathering places.

Pedestal water features provide a perfect setting for landscape art.

Elevated spas add to the casual lifestyle of any pool.

The straight lines of this contemporary design lead you to a thatched cover kitchen and swim-up bar.

WetFlame fire elements are striking against the dark, multi-colored tile and decking.

Wrap around wet deck and bench provide for an abundance of in-pool lounging space.

The large raised water feature and fire elements can be enjoyed from both the raised spa and the seat wall.

Landscape art takes center stage among the cana lily.

This 256 square foot Pixie Pool boasts
six water features, two fire pots and a
spa spillway.

This L-shaped pool provides a view from any angle in the home.

Colored lighting in the pool, spa and
fountain add to the night ambiance.

A terraced pool and spa take
advantage of the natural landscape.

Diamond shaped pedestal water
features bookend the wok pot
fire element.

Unique water elements and decking materials accentuate contemporary styling in these pools.

A dramatic look is achieved in this Pixie Pool with dark covered pads, pedestals and tile.

Flagstone accents are incorporated in the water wall, dam walls and coping.

On The Edge

Designs that incorporate a knife edge beam
for the illusion of an endless flow of water

One of the most spectacular effects one can integrate into the design of a pool is an infinity edge. However, there are certain conditions that need to be present to realize the total benefit of the design.

By definition, an infinity edge pool is one with a visual effect of the water flowing seamlessly to the horizon.

The dynamics of the infinity edge pool are the result of precise hydraulic and architectural design. Hydraulically, the equipment must draw enough water from the catch basin to raise the pool water level enough to overflow and cascade over the entire length of the dam wall, so that the edge of the dam wall disappears. Architecturally, the pool must be strategically positioned in the yard so that the line-of-sight from the deck or the interior of the home captures the visual effect created by the infinity edge.

Infinity edge pools were originally created for coast line homes where the view of the horizon was an ocean, lake or other waterways.

The dramatic visuals created by an infinity edge pool have become so popular that it has inspired designers to incorporate the special effect in all types of landscapes.

There are however, certain essential conditions that need to be present before one decides to integrate an infinity edge in the pool. A drop off in the lot elevation and an unobstructed or a semi-obstructed horizon are necessary.

There are a few techniques designers can use to enhance the circumstances, one of which would be to raise the pool partially out-of-ground creating the required elevation change needed for the effect.

Another consideration is the view from the backside of the pool. In most cases, one isn't concerned with the backside of the dam wall and trough, since this is not typically a focal point of the pool. However, in larger yards where some of the activities take place beyond the backside of the pool, then consideration must be given to the final overall look and desired water effect.

Variations of the infinity edge are achieved by reversing the infinity edge so that the water flows towards the house or to incorporate two or more sides of the pool as an infinity edge. An elevation change is still required with any of these variations.

One can also create interesting water features by changing the profile and textures of the vertical plane of the dam wall with tiles, natural stones and boulders.

A cliff above a golf course provides an ideal setting for this infinity edge pool and spa.

An infinity edge spa is designed inside the pool.

A long offset infinity edge is accented
with a random pattern multi-colored tile.

Picture book corners are the only interruption in this perimeter overflow design.

This infinity edge pool was added to an existing spa.

The freeform infinity edge is dotted with boulders.

Black pebble interior and charcoal tile add a mysterious aura to this pool.

This three tiered infinity edge pool
is framed with natural slate tiles.

Sea life mosaics add a
lighthearted feeling to this
infinity edge.

The entire pool was raised 18 inches out of ground to dramatize the arched infinity edge.

Therapeutic Havens

Designs that transform typical spas
into hydrotherapy baths and healing retreats

Nothing relieves stress better than spending a day at the spa being pampered, relaxing in hydrotherapy baths, breathing in the aromatic fragrances of eucalyptus and lavender, sipping on citrus infused water and listening to calming sounds. But time constraints, work schedules and family activities prevent you from indulging at your favorite spa getaway. By the time you scrape together a few hours for yourself, the spa is closed for the evening or the babysitter is unavailable.

There are plenty of backyard spas sitting idle and under-used across the globe; with a few tips your backyard spa can be transformed into a luxury therapeutic haven or the site for the latest themed gathering, the "Spa Social."

Water is the basic element of any thorough spa experience, both externally and internally. The healing powers of water and hydrotherapy baths date back to ancient Rome. In addition to massages and facials, a modern day, full service, luxury spa offers ritual or wet areas providing additional amenities to enhance the relaxation factor, with multiple hydrotherapy baths, saunas and vichey showers. Hydrotherapy tubs claim remedies for everything from day-to-day stress to headaches, hangovers, over exercised muscles, fatigue, and jet lag.

There is more to indulging in a spa than simply soaking in a heated, bubbling aqueous basin. A comprehensive spa environment stimulating all the senses is what makes the spa encounter complete. Here are some ideas for preparing the spa and conceiving your own ritual area, making those few stolen moments feel like a top rated spa experience.

Assemble a basket of spa essentials in advance to ensure that you are fully equipped for that moment when you can slip away. Some essential spa items to include are sandals, a robe, aromatherapy candles, lighter, facial and bath towels, a variety of spa products in different fragrances, CDs, CD player, eye and neck pillows.

Preheat the spa while you are gathering a few other items: a pitcher of chilled water with citrus slices, iced face towels and cucumber slices (for your eyes). Wet the face towels in ice water, roll and place on a tray along with the sliced cucumbers and ice cubes to keep them cool. Light the candles and arrange the items around the spa within arms reach for easy accessibility.

The audio element is just as important as other spa components. Soothing background music with a melody of sounds, water environments or nature tunes further enhance the therapeutic mood.

Hydrating one's body internally is vital during any therapeutic encounter. Drinking detoxifying and anti-oxidant beverages will further the benefits of the spa experience. Hot organic teas, chilled water with citrus slices and fruit juices are perfect spa thirst quenchers.

Take the spa experience to another level by participating in an invigorating hot/cold plunge. Move back and forth from the heated hot tub to the cool waters of the swimming pool several times to stimulate circulation. Ideal temperatures are 100-102 degrees Fahrenheit for the hot plunge and 68-72 degrees Fahrenheit for the cold plunge.

To create more spa appeal in your ritual area, intertwine sheer draping through wrought iron garden accessories, place large bouquets of fresh fragrant flowers around the spa, and incorporate soft lighting with tinted lenses or colored lights to add a romantic and calm ambiance.

Now that you have a personal at-home ritual area and spa basket, you may want to schedule a regular spa day on a weekly or monthly basis. Or consider throwing a *Spa Social*™ for your next gathering or fundraiser. For additional entertainment, hire a masseuse or two to provide foot, neck and body massages for the guests.

Transform the spa into a therapeutic haven.

Attached or stand-alone spas can be customized
into any shape, size and style.

Natural stones and tiles create an alluring setting.

Emphasize the spa area by creating an elevation.

Inferno Infatuation

Embellishments that harness
the dazzling mystique and beauty of fire

Mankind has been infatuated with fire since its discovery a million years ago. The ability to control such a powerful, self-sustaining and dangerous force for the benefit of our survival is intriguing.

The dance of the flames can be mesmerizing, and with the reflective qualities of water, mixing the two together creates a rare euphoric aura. Inferno themed features provide entertainment, light and heat, enhancing the backyard living experience, extending it into the evening hours and throughout the seasons. For many homeowners fire has become a must-have on their wish list.

Several years ago I introduced the *WetFlame*™, a combination water and fire element with a pool designed for a custom home showcased in a luxury home tour. The striking contrast between fire and water make for an intriguing ambiance. Incorporating these opposing forces into one harmonious entity created an unforeseen craze. Pool designers from all over the globe began using versions of the *WetFlame*™ in some fashion with their designs.

Dual WetFlames and a sheer descent create an alluring feature on this crescent-shaped pool.

Raised fire pits can be styled and finished in a variety of ways.

Deck level fire pits can be filled with multi-colored tempered glass, lava rock or fire rated stone.

Built-in seat walls create an inviting place to sit.

An open hearth is a dramatic edition to any backyard.

Culinary Corner

The evolution of cooking outdoors has reached new heights; it is no longer the man of the house standing alone over a hibachi or portable gas grill. Now it's the whole family showing off their cooking skills in an elaborate outdoor kitchen next to the pool, preparing recipes learned from their favorite cooking show, and truly living the *al fresco* lifestyle year round.

All the conveniences of the home can be brought poolside with outdoor-friendly appliances designed to deal with heat, cold and other adverse weather elements. Large cooking grills feature multi-levels with six or more burners, warming trays and side burners to cook everything from roasts to vegetables. No kitchen would be complete without an ice maker, refrigerator or wet bar. And, the latest trend is open-hearth pizza ovens.

The entertainment and cooking areas are an extension of the pool and in many cases actually become a part of the pool, with swim-up bars and raised or sunken outdoor kitchens that share a common wall with the pool.

Swim-up, peninsula and island bars with permanent pedestal seats allow swimmers a place to sit and enjoy refreshments without exiting the pool. Designing these bars adjacent to the outdoor kitchen makes it even more convenient for service and allows guests to interact with the host, chef or bartender. This type of swim-up bar is a popular hangout at resort hotel pools and is making its way into the backyard.

Built-in seat walls showing off colorful pillows and cushions provide a vibrant background and additional seating for large gatherings, eliminating the need for folding chairs.

Even if the outdoor kitchen or electronic elements will be added after the pool is built, planning in advance can save future expenses. Electric and gas lines can be designed and installed during the construction of the pool and hooked up at a later date.

This custom designed outdoor kitchen boasts a double grill, chiller, refrigerator, hearth and a extended bar for guest seating.

A pergola provides shade
for this outdoor eatery.

This large sunken kitchen
features a swim up bar.

Drapery provides shelter from
the sun in this poolside kitchen.

A large swim-up counter provides seating for four.

The outdoor kitchen is shaded by an arbor.

This south Pacific kitchen and bar is well equipped to serve guests.

A round granite table resides within this large curved culinary setting.

This kitchen features plenty of storage space.

The culinary center is conveniently placed next to the stone patio.

This spacious
kitchen features
a large wet bar,
numerous cabinets,
and a refrigerator.

This fully equipped, step-down
kitchen features a swim-up bar.

The position of this culinary center
allows the cook to oversee the
activities in the pool.

A wood fired pizza oven is the main attraction of this Mexican styled kitchen.

A palapa provides shade from the sun.

Engaging Events

Backyards often get ignored when it comes to decorating for the holidays or celebrations. Moving to the pool area for these special occasions allows one to enjoy the beauty of the pool year-round, creating enchanting, fun, memorable and engaging events.

Quality décor that can be used year-after-year is available at party stores, costume outlets, theatrical supply stores, seasonal retail displays, pool supply stores and home improvements stores.

Take time to develop the theme and plan the setting before you purchase the décor. Determine a focal point to draw your guest's attention and then create pathways to allow access to key areas. The pool can be the focal point or simply compliment the water-themed setting.

This pool turned Pirate's Cove with its riches is guarded by beautiful, ghostly, siren pirates. Numerous unsuspecting trespassers have met their demise while attempting to steal the treasures.

Backyard pools and spas are beautiful sites for weddings, receptions and bridal photos.

Pre-lit trees and motion deer around the pool
are magnified by the reflection in the water.

Valentines Day becomes a private
intimate affair in the backyard spa.

Light and water activated floating
lights add ambiance and a colorful
décor to poolside activities.

Grilling Like a Master Chef

Recipes from Certified Master Chef Gustav Mauler

Who best to provide insight on celebrating the *al fresco* lifestyle than renowned restaurateur and Certified Master Chef, Gustav Mauler. His acclaimed Las Vegas restaurant, Spiedini, features a large *al fresco* dining area amidst lush waterfalls with koi, lavish landscaping, and an occasional flock of ducks. This outdoor space is frequently booked for private parties, weddings and receptions with delicacies provided by his own Gustav's Master Catering.

A native Austrian, Gustav E. Mauler, CMC is President and CEO of Gustav International, a restaurant, hospitality, management and design consulting firm. He is one of a few who have attained the highly coveted designation of Certified Master Chef from the American Culinary Federation.

His move to Nevada in 1987 impacted the dining scene in Las Vegas forever, paving the way for independent restaurateurs and celebrity chefs to open fashionable Las Vegas eateries. As Senior Vice President with Mirage Resorts, Mauler oversaw the development, planning and design of a myriad of restaurants, lounges and convention areas for multiple properties. He worked with local health authorities in recommending food standards now in effect for the county.

His culinary achievements are vast. A highly sought after personality, Gustav makes appearances across the globe; performing culinary demonstrations on luxury cruises, at celebrity affairs, for television broadcasts, international food & wine events and charity causes as well as contributing to many publications.

"In my numerous adventures and chef positions around the globe, I have found that people truly enjoy dining outdoors. Many of the finest resorts in the world feature *al fresco* dining, and the most sought after seats are clearly those adjacent to pools and water features," notes Mauler.

Gustav graciously shares a few grilling tips and a selection of his famed recipes to assist you in becoming a master of the grill! To learn more about Gustav go to www.gustavinternational.com.

Grilling Tips

The secret to outdoor grilling is practice, patience and preparation.

Think of the barbecue as a secondary oven or grill. This will allow you more flexibility with time and preparation for any meal.

Purchase the appropriate grilling tools: utensils with long wooden covered handles, well-fitting mitts and water squirt bottle to calm down flames created from grease and drippings.

Do not place raw chicken on the same plate with other meats.

Frequently wash hands with soap and water when handling foods especially chicken or other fowl.

Timing is everything when it comes to grilling.

Always start with the larger pieces and with foods that need to cook longer such as briskets, large steaks, and chicken breast with bone, then move on to smaller portions and vegetables.

Always have both a high and a medium to low flame when grilling. Use the high flame to create that charred look on foods and finish the cooking process on the lower heat.

Watch the temperature of the grill, the more food you cook the quicker you will use up the heat. This is even more significant when cooking with charcoal and wood.

Most people tend to over-cook food when grilling, so remember that you can always put the food back on to the grill and cook it more if it's not to the liking of you and your guests.

Never place cooked meats on the same tray that was used in preparing and transporting the raw food. Get a clean dish to serve the food.

When you've finished cooking leave the grill on for a short time to burn off any residue from the food, this will sanitize the grill for future cooking.

Beef is one of the most common foods cooked on the grill. The best meats are ground beef for burgers, and tri-tip for skewering and sliced steak. For steaks use filet, New York and rib eye with rib eye being the juiciest.

Prepare a menu that stands out from the ordinary barbeque fare.

Grill Roasted Turkey

serves twelve

sage butter and giblet gravy
2 gallons cold water
1 cup plus 2 teaspoons coarse kosher salt
1 cup packed golden brown sugar
2 tablespoon whole black peppercorns
6 whole bay leaves
5 sprigs fresh rosemary
1 20 to 22 pound turkey, reserve neck, heart, and gizzard for gravy
5 cups hickory wood chips, soaked in water 1 hour and drained
1 to 3 disposable aluminum broiler pans
1 and 1/4 cup butter, room temperature
1/3 cup chopped fresh sage
2 celery stalks, cut into 1 inch pieces
1 onion, peeled and quartered
2 cups dry white wine

Stir 2 gallons water, 1 cup salt, sugar, peppercorns, bay leaves, and rosemary in large bowl until salt and sugar dissolve. Line large pot with two 33-gallon plastic bags, placing one inside the other. Place turkey in bag-lined pot, breast side down. Pour brine over turkey; press to submerge. Twist tops of bags to eliminate air pockets and secure. Refrigerate turkey in brine 24 hours. Drain turkey; discard brine. Rinse turkey; pat dry. Blend 1/4 cup butter and sage in small bowl; season with pepper. Starting at neck end, slide hand between skin and breast meat to loosen skin. Spread sage butter over breast meat and skin.

Sprinkle cavities with salt and pepper. Stuff main cavity with celery and onion. Fold wing tips under, tie legs together. Melt 1 cup butter over low heat. Remove from heat, whisk in wine. Place turkey in center of grill rack, breast side up, above empty broiler pan. Brush turkey generously with butter-wine basting mixture. Cover barbecue. Cook until thermometer inserted into thickest part of thigh registers 165°f, basting with butter-wine mixture and adding 1 cup drained wood chips (and 6 briquettes if using charcoal barbecue) every 30 minutes, about 3 hours total. Cover top of turkey with foil if browning too quickly. Transfer turkey to platter. Tent loosely with foil; let stand 30 minutes, internal temperature will increase 5 to 10 degrees. Serve turkey with Giblet Gravy.

Charcoal Barbecue

Mound charcoal briquettes in barbecue on lower grill rack; burn until light gray. Using tongs, carefully divide hot briquettes into 2 piles, 1 pile at each side of rack. Sprinkle each pile with 1/2 cup drained soaked hickory chips. Place empty broiler pan between piles. Position upper grill rack at least 6 inches above briquettes. Adjust barbecue vents so that chips smoke and briquettes burn but do not flame.

Certified Master Chef Gustav Mauler prepares and serves a traditional Thanksgiving turkey outdoors.

Gas or Electric Barbecue

Preheat barbecue with all burners on high. Turn off center burner; reduce outside burners to medium-low. Place 1/2 cup drained soaked hickory chips in each of 2 broiler pans. Set pans over 2 lit burners. Place empty broiler pan under grill rack over unlit burner. Position grill racks at least 6 inches above burners.

Giblet Gravy

makes 3 1/2 cups

neck, heart, and gizzard reserved from turkey
4 cups (or more) low-salt chicken broth
1/2 cup chopped onion
1/2 cup chopped celery
1/4 cup butter (half stick)
1/4 cup all purpose flour
1/4 cup whipping cream

Combine turkey neck, heart, and gizzard, 4 cups broth, onion, and celery in large saucepan; bring to boil. Reduce heat to medium, cover. Simmer until neck and gizzard are tender, about 35 minutes. Transfer turkey parts to work surface; cool. Chop gizzard and heart. Pull meat from neck; chop finely. Strain giblet broth into large glass measuring cup. Add more chicken broth if necessary to measure 3 1/4 cups. Melt butter in heavy medium saucepan over medium heat. Add flour, stir until golden, about 5 minutes. Whisk in broth mixture, then cream. Bring to boil, whisking until smooth. Add giblets and neck meat. Cook until thick enough to coat spoon, stirring often, about 8 minutes. Season with salt and pepper.

Prosciutto and Melon

serves four
8 slices prosciutto (thinly sliced)
1/2 honeydew or cantaloupe melon
8 strawberries

    Rinse and prepare strawberries and melon. Layer melon and strawberries.
    Roll prosciutto and place across fruit. Pepper to taste.

Prosciutto and Melon

Grilling Like a Master Chef

Chopped Salad

serves eight

2 heads romaine lettuce (outer leavers removed) thinly sliced
2 ears corn on the cob (cooked for 5 minutes & nicely charred or grilled at the outside, remove kernels from husk)
1/4 cup carrots finely diced
1/4 cup zucchini finely diced
1/2 cup tomato finely diced
8 slices bacon (cooked crisp & finely chopped)

3/4 cup Russian dressing
4 ripe avocados, pitted, peeled and scored
2 potatoes cut in fine julienne strips, crispy fried

Assemble in a four-inch wide by two-inch tall ring molds. First layer; mix romaine with 1/2 cup Russian dressing, place in ring mold. Mix second layer: chopped vegetables and corn kernels with 1/4 cup Russian dressing. Third layer: sprinkle chopped crispy bacon. Fourth layer: half an avocado spread out evenly. Top with crispy potato straws.

Chopped Salad

Roma Tomatoes with Bleu Cheese

serves six to eight

1 head lettuce, washed, dried and chopped
6 to 8 ripe roma tomatoes, sliced
1 cup crumbled bleu cheese
1 cup fresh basil leaves, cut into ribbons

Dressing:
3 tablespoons balsamic vinegar
1/4 cup olive oil
2 tablespoons sugar
1 small garlic clove, crushed
1/2 teaspoon salt

Make the dressing in a glass jar with a tight-fitting lid, combine the dressing ingredients and shake well. Keep chilled until ready to use. Arrange the lettuce on a large platter. Distribute the tomato slices, bleu cheese and basil attractively over the lettuce. Drizzle the dressing over the salad just before serving.

Roma Tomatoes with Bleu Cheese

Spiedini Spinach Salad

serves four
1 fresh pear
16 ounces baby spinach
4 ounces bleu cheese crumbles
4 thin slices of prosciutto crispy baked
1/2 cup candied walnuts

Balsamic vinaigrette dressing:
1/3 cup red wine vinegar
1/2 cup balsamic vinegar
1 tablespoon soy sauce

2 tablespoons dijon mustard
1/2 tablespoon shallots, minced
1/2 tablespoon blanched garlic, minced
to taste, salt
to taste, ground black pepper
1/2 cup olive oil
1/2 cup canola oil

In a clean mixing bowl, combine all ingredients except oils. Add oils slowly, mixing until all the ingredients are thoroughly blended and lightly emulsified. Transfer to clean container. Cover, date and store.

Spiedini Spinach Salad

Potato Salad with Arugula

2 pounds new potatoes
1/2 pound yellow onions
1/2 cup olive oil
1/4 cup vinegar
1 cup warm water
2 tablespoons dijon mustard
1 tablespoon sugar
to taste, salt and pepper
2 cups arugula

Boil Potatoes for 20 minutes until tender. Then Drain.

Dressing:

Mix vinegar, oil, warm water, sugar, and mustard, salt and pepper well. Cut potatoes in quarters when warm. Add to dressing and mix. (adding warm potatoes will give it a creamy consistency). Before serving taste for seasoning again, then add arugula just before serving.

Potato Salad with Arugula

Grilling Like a Master Chef

Steak and Bleu Cheese Salad

serves four

two 8 oz choice steaks, well trimmed (cook to your
    liking)
to taste, salt and pepper
2 each romaine hearts
1 medium red onion, sliced in rings
1/2 cup cherry tomatoes

Dressing:
1/2 cup California raisins
1/2 cup mayonnaise

1 teaspoon minced shallots
1 teaspoon minced garlic
2 tablespoons chopped parsley
4 ounces bleu cheese, crumbled
1/2 cup buttermilk
to taste, kosher salt
1/2 lemon, juiced

Divide romaine leaves among four dinner plates
and spoon dressing on each salad. Thinly slice steak
and arrange on the dressed romaine. Garnish with
onion rings and cherry tomatoes.

Steak and Bleu Cheese Salad

Bleu Cheese Burgers

serves five
2 pounds fresh ground beef (85% lean)
10 ounces bleu cheese
4 ounce can tomato juice
to taste, salt and pepper

Mix above ingredients. Shape into 5-6 ounce patties. Create a well in center and fill with 1/2 ounce bleu cheese. Close and shape with hands dipped in water to achieve a smooth patty. Grill the burgers to your liking.

Bleu Cheese Burgers

Pecan Crusted Lamb Chops

serves two

six 4-ounce Frenched lamb chops
2 tablespoons olive oil
1/2 cup chopped pecans
4 tablespoons dijon mustard
1 tablespoon honey
to taste, salt and pepper

Season lamb chops with salt and pepper. Mix dijon mustard and honey, brush on both sides of chops. Dip lamb chops in the chopped pecans to coat. Heat 2 table-spoons of oil in a large sauté pan over medium to high heat. Carefully lay 6 chops in the pan and sear for 6 minutes or until a crisp crust has formed. Carefully turn and sear for 6 more minutes on the other side or until a crust has formed and lamb has cooked to medium rare. Criss-cross lamb chops on center of each plate and add your preferred accompaniments.

Pecan Crusted Lamb Chops

Honey-Glazed Salmon
with Pineapple Salsa

serves four
4 6-ounce salmon filets

Marinade:
1 tablespoon honey
1 tablespoon teriyaki sauce
1 tablespoon pineapple sauce
1 clove garlic

Place the salmon filets in a re-sealable plastic bag. Combine the marinade ingredients in a glass bowl or measuring cup. Pour the marinade over the filets, seal the bag, and refrigerate for at least 1 hour. On a hot grill sprayed with vegetable oil cooking spray, grill the salmon skin side down over hot coals. Watch for the fish to cook from the bottom up, it takes about 12 to 15 minutes. Serve with Pineapple Salsa.

Marinated Filet Mignon

serves six
6 small filet mignon beef steaks (approximately 1 1/2 to 2 inches thick)

Marinade:
1/2 cup olive oil
1 clove garlic, crushed
2 teaspoons finely chopped fresh rosemary
2 teaspoons finely chopped fresh thyme
1 lemon juiced

Place the filets in a re-sealable plastic bag. Combine the marinade ingredients in a glass bowl or measuring cup. Pour the marinade over the filets, seal the bag, and refrigerate for at least 1 hour or overnight. When ready to cook, place the filets over hot coals and grill for about 10 minutes per side or until the internal temperature is between 125 degrees and 130 degrees (medium rare).

Lemon & Herb Chicken Breast

serves four
4 6 to 8 ounce chicken breasts
1 lemon, juiced
2 tablespoons olive oil
1 tablespoon finely chopped rosemary
to taste, salt & pepper

Mix the olive oil, rosemary, lemon juice, salt and pepper in small bowl. Place chicken breasts in a large bowl, pour marinade over chicken breasts then cover with plastic wrap. Store in the refrigerator for a few hours. When ready to cook, position the chicken over indirect heat and grill at medium heat until cooked through, until juices run clear. Approximately 18 to 22 minutes, depending on the thickness of the breast.

Lemon and Herb Chicken Breast, Marinated Filet Mignon, and Honey-Glazed Salmon

Grilling Like a Master Chef

Thai Grilled Shrimp Skewer

serves four
16 jumbo shrimp
1/2 cup crushed pineapple
1/4 cup seeded, finely diced green peppers
1 thinly sliced scallion
1 pinch chili powder
1/4 teaspoon course salt
to taste, ground pepper

Preheat grill and light half hour before grilling. Using a paring knife, butterfly the shrimp lengthwise down the middle. Rinse well. Dry on paper towels. In a medium bowl combine pineapple, green pepper, scallion, chili powder, salt and pepper. Fill each shrimp with 1 tablespoon of stuffing. Slide 4 shrimp on a skewer and cook on grill for 3 minutes each side or until pale pink.

Barbecue Spiced Lamb Skewer and Salsa

serves six
2 pounds boned lamb leg
1 lime, juiced

2 garlic cloves
3/4 cup plain yogurt
1/2 teaspoon ground coriander
1/2 teaspoon ground cumin
1/4 teaspoon chili powder
1/4 teaspoon ground ginger
to taste, salt

Salsa:
2 small red onions diced
4 seeded and diced ripe plum tomatoes
3 ounces chopped cilantro leaves
1/2 teaspoon sugar
to taste, ground pepper

Trim the lamb and cut in 1 1/2-inch cubes. In a bowl, add salt and lime juice to lamb. Mix and add yogurt and remaining spices. Marinate over night or at least 6 hours. Preheat barbecue and skewer meat. Grill at a high temperature for 5 minutes each side to give a nice charred finish. Let sit for a few minutes before serving with red onions, tomato and lime salsa. The use of yogurt as a tenderizing marinade is common throughout the Middle East and Indian subcontinents.

Thai Grilled Shrimp and Barbeque Spiced Lamb

Mediterranean Tuna

serves two

2 6-ounce Ahi tuna steaks
6 tablespoons extra virgin olive oil
to taste kosher salt
to taste fresh ground pepper
6 ounce fingerling potatoes
2 roma tomatoes, slowly roasted
1/2 fennel, sliced thin
1 cup arugula
6 nicoise olives
1/2 lemon

Boil fingerling potatoes, cut into 1/4-inch slices, sauté quickly. Season with salt and pepper. Slice roma tomatoes in half, slowly roast at 275 degrees. Drizzle with 3 tablespoons extra virgin olive oil and kosher salt. In a small sauté pan, over high heat, add 2 tablespoons olive oil. Season tuna with salt and pepper. Sear tuna filets until all sides are brown, keeping center rare, about 1 to 2 minutes. Toss arugula and shaved fennel with juice of lemon and 1 tablespoon olive oil. Arrange fingerling potatoes, top with a few slices of tuna, crown with fennel. Garnish with roasted tomatoes and olives.

Mediterranean Tuna

Grilling Like a Master Chef

Tuna Tataki Salad

serves four

16-ounce Ahi tuna
1/4 cup sesame seed
2 tablespoon crushed black pepper
1/4 teaspoon ginger
to taste, kosher salt
4 ounces olive oil
1 lime, juiced
1/4 cup soy sauce
1 shallot, chopped
2 cups greens salad mix
fennel

Mix sesame seeds, black pepper, kosher salt, and touch of ginger. Heat 2 tablespoons olive oil. Roll tuna in sesame seed and black pepper, sear quickly in hot pan on all sides. For the salad dressing, mix olive oil, lime juice, soy sauce, salt, pepper and shallots. Drizzle over salad and tuna. Garnish with shaved fennel.

Tuna Tataki Salad

Tuna Tartare

3 ounces sushi-grade tuna, diced in 3/8-inch size,
    keep chilled
2 tablespoons chili oil
1 pinch, fresh ginger
to taste, fresh ground pepper and sea salt
dash of Tabasco
1/8 avocado, finely diced
radish sprouts

Fill bottom bowl with ice, place a bowl on top. In top bowl mix tuna with 1 tablespoon of chili oil, ginger, fresh pepper, sea salt and a dash of Tabasco. Arrange on plate in a 2 or 3 inch cookie cutter, top with avocado and radish sprouts. Drizzle 1 tablespoon chili oil on plate, garnish with a few twists of fresh pepper.

Tuna Tartare

Tuna Carpaccio

serves one

4 ounces thinly sliced big-eye tuna
1/2 ounce virgin olive oil
to taste, kosher salt or sea salt
to taste, freshly ground pepper

2 shaved radishes
few springs fresh chive, chopped

Pound tuna slices thin, between plastic wrap. Drizzle with olive oil, salt and pepper to taste and garnish with radishes and chives.

Tuna Carpaccio

Flat Bread (pizza) Dough

yields 2 large or 4 small pizzas
3 cup all purpose flour
1 teaspoon salt
1 teaspoon honey
1 tablespoon olive oil
1 packet dry yeast
1 cup warm water
1/2 teaspoon sugar

Dissolve the yeast, honey and sugar in 1 cup of warm water. In a mixer fitted with a dough hook, combine flour and salt. Mix on low speed, then add the yeast mixture and oil and mix for approx 5 minutes. Place the dough on a clean surface. Cover with a damp towel and let rise for 30 minutes. Divide the dough into 2 or 4 balls. Work and roll the balls until smooth and firm. Cover the balls with a damp towel and let rest for 15 minutes. Roll each ball in flour, shaking off any excess. Place the balls on a lightly floured surface and stretch the dough with a rolling pin until about 16 inches in diameter (for large). Place dough on pizza tray. Cover with sauce, mozzarella cheese and toppings. Bake in 400-degree oven for 12-15 minutes.

Tip: You can make the dough up to 2 days ahead. Wrap balls loosely in a damp towel, place in a plastic bag and put in the refrigerator until ready to use.

Suggested toppings: pepperoni, sausage, Canadian bacon, mushrooms, onion, green peppers, pineapple, black olives.

Gourmet toppings: shrimp, lobster, anchovies, asparagus, roasted red peppers or jalapenos.

Specialty flat breads: Spinach flat bread, mozzarella and ricotta cheese topped with spinach. White-out flat bread, eliminate the sauce and cover with four types of white cheese: mozzarella, fontana, parmesan and ricotta.

Pizza Sauce

4 cups tomato sauce
1 tablespoon sugar
1/4 teaspoon black pepper
1 tablespoon chopped garlic
1 tablespoon dried oregano
1 tablespoon salt
1 tablespoon dried basil

Mix all ingredients in a food processor until smooth. Cover and refrigerate until ready for use.

Flat Bread (Pizza)

Watermelon Coconut Napoleon

serves four

1/2 small seedless watermelon
1 cup shredded sweetened coconut
1 1/2 cups fresh raspberries
2 shots Malibu Coconut Rum

Cut 1/2 inch thick slices of watermelon using a 4 inch round cutter, cutting 12 round disks, and reserve remaining watermelon. Place a watermelon disk on plate. Top with coconut and raspberry. Repeat layers. Top with remaining watermelon slices. Garnish with a spoonful of coconut and a few raspberries. Use half shot of Malibu Coconut Rum to soak the napoleon. Served chilled.

Watermelon Coconut Napoleon

Classic Strawberries Romanoff

serves four
1 cup strawberries
1 tablespoon sugar
2 scoops vanilla low-fat ice cream or yogurt, softened slightly
1/2 cup reduced or non-fat whipped topping or whipped cream product
2 teaspoons chocolate shavings
1 1/2 ounces Grand Marnier

Prepare the strawberries by washing thoroughly, removing the stems, and cutting in half. Place in medium mixing bowl and sprinkle with sugar. Add Grand Marnier and mix lightly, allow to marinate for 10 minutes. Fold in yogurt or ice cream and whipped topping. Serve in a frozen martini glass with chocolate shavings as garnish.

Classic Strawberries Romanoff

Ginger Peach Tea

yields one pitcher
1 ginger root
Tea bags or leaves
1 fresh peach

Place large chunks or slices of fresh peaches into ice cube tray, add water and freeze. In cold water add 1 inch fresh ginger root, shaved. Bring to a boil, add tea leaves or bags and steep to desired strength, chill. Pour over peach ice cubes, add a dollop of peach nectar, stir and serve. Garnish with a slice of fresh ginger root

Cucumber Water

Ginger Peach Tea

Cucumber Water

yields one pitcher
tap or bottled sparkling or non-sparkling water
1 large cucumber

Slice cucumber (skin on) into thin discs. Place half of the slices into the bottom of a large glass pitcher. Fill with ice and water. Place cucumber slices in each water glass and one on rim of glass. Pour when ready to serve.

Caribbean Cooler

serves one
1 cup cold milk
1/2 banana, cut up
1/4 cup frozen orange juice concentrate

Blend until smooth, garnish with a slice of banana (peel on)

Caribbean Cooler

Poolside Potions

Alcoholic or not, chilled drinks seem to taste better when you're relaxing by the pool. One of Las Vegas' revered Mixologist, Shawn Barker, shares a few of his trade skills to assist you in becoming the entertainment and focal point of the party with some distinctive poolside drinkable potions.

A bartender for Wolfgang Puck's Bar and Grill in the MGM Hotel and Casino, Shawn's resume includes stints at some of Las Vegas' most celebrated restaurants and nightclubs including Wolfgang's Chinois, Mist Bar & Lounge, Caramel, the Foundation Room and the now closed ICE. Shawn's keen sense of blending flavors, spirits and juices has resulted in some very popular concoctions featured on specialty drink menus.

Barker adds his own twist to traditional cocktail favorites and trendy drinks including the Bloody Mary, Martinis, Sake, and the hottest cocktail of the season the Mojito.

"Cocktails are like good wines. They need to have balance and structure. Sweetness, citrus, and fruit should not be overpowering but inviting. And don't over pour on the liquor; in many cases it will change the flavor of the drink," states Barker. "The mark of a good bartender is consistency. You must be able to make the same drink over and over again and have it taste the same each time."

He suggests developing a theme around the party, using décor, exotic garnishes, or simply changing the names of the drinks you already know how to make to coincide with the theme. Then print a menu with a list of the poolside potions you are serving.

For a professional appearance, Shawn advises the host to prep the bar, as one would prep the food. Cut all the garnishes and fruit in advance and refrigerate. Don't forget straws, swizzle sticks, cocktail pics, napkins, ice, and glassware. High-grade acrylic glasses come in a variety of sizes, shapes and colors and appear much like real glass containers. To minimize confusion of what beverage is alcoholic or alcohol-free, use different glasses to serve each. For example, use bright, smoky colored glasses for the non-alcoholic and clear acrylic for those with liquor.

He also recommends arranging canned and bottled (plastic) beverages in an open ice bath (2/3 ice and 1/3 water) close at hand for easy access. Outdoors, ice melts quickly so always have lots of extra ice available. And, NEVER use a glass container to scoop ice from a bucket, bin or ice chest. If the glass breaks, the entire batch of ice must be discarded!

"Mojitos and Caipirinha are popular drinks and even now I find a lot of bartenders don't make the drink correctly," notes Barker, who has over ten years bartending experience. "Never use a pre-made Mojito mix, drinks always taste better when you put a little love into them." Some of the keys to making a proper Mojito is using RAW cane sugar. The beverage should be crisp, clean and not too sweet. And learn to muddle well. Using the flat knobbed side of the muddler in the glass, press the fruits and herbs by rotating your wrist in a downward motion.

For layered potions, Barker says to refrigerate liqueurs such as Blue Curacao to change the viscosity and density of the liquid, allowing you to float or sink the liqueur for a colorful cocktail.

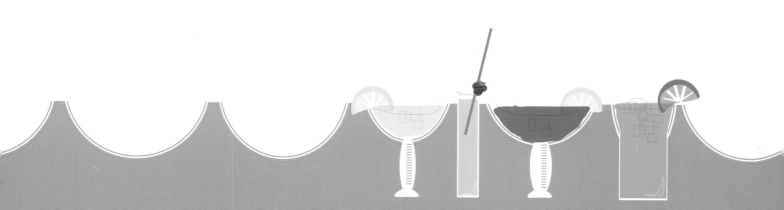

And lastly, Barker claims the most important aspect of being a bartender is to have fun. You are the creator of the specialty potions, the focal point of the party so enjoy what you are doing!

Mixologist Shawn Barker pours his specialty potions for his poolside guest, Ashley.

Barker's specialty drinks; Caipirinha, Mandarin Mojito, Forbidden Beach, and Pomegranate Paradise

Poolside Potions by Mixologist Shawn Barker

Caipirinha

1 teaspoon raw cane sugar
1 lime
2 ounces cachaca Brazilian rum

In an old-fashion glass muddle sugar and lime with a splash of soda. Add ice to fill glass, add cachaca, stir, garnish with lime wheel.

Mandarin Mojito

1 1/2 ounces orange rum
1/2 wedged lime
1/2 teaspoon raw cane sugar
6-8 mint sprigs (no stems)
1/2 mandarin orange
3 ounces soda water

In a tall glass add mint, lime, orange, sugar, and a splash of soda water. Muddle. Very important to press oil out of mint, along with crushing the sugar. Add ice to fill glass. Add rum, top with soda water, turn. Garnish with a mint sprig or an orange wedge. Can also be made non-alcoholic by omitting the rum.

Forbidden Beach

1/2 ounce Stoli Strasberi vodka
1/2 ounce gin
1/2 ounce rum
1/2 ounce triple sec
2 ounces sweet & sour mix
2 ounces cranberry juice
dash of strawberry daiquiri mix

Fill tall glass with ice. Put liquor ingredients in followed by juices. Stir. Garnish with lemon wedge. This drink can also be made as a non-alcoholic Strawberry Lemonade. Fill tall glass with ice. Add 4 ounces lemonade, 2 ounces cranberry, 2 ounces sweet and sour, a splash of strawberry daiquiri mix, and soda water or sprite.

Pomegranate Paradise

1 ounce vodka
1 ounce Pama liqueur
1/2 ounce amaretto
1/2 ounce sweet and sour mix
1/4 fresh orange, squeeze

Put all ingredients into shaker glass. Fill with ice. Shake vigorously approximately 20 times. Strain into martini glass or over ice in an old-fashion glass. Garnished with an orange twist.

Frozen Emerald Melon Ball

1 ounce vodka
1 ounce midori
2 ounce fresh orange juice
splash of pineapple
1/2 ounce Blue Curacao

Put vodka, Midori, orange juice, pineapple into blender with ice. Blend, pour into goblet and top with blue Curacao. Stir. Garnish with cherry wrapped in orange wedge. Keep Blue Curacao in refrigerator to make liquor more viscous.

Ginger Peach Bellini

1/2 teaspoon minced ginger
1/2 ounce peach schnapps
splash cranberry (for color)
1/2 ounce peach puree
3 ounces sparkling wine or champagne

Mix ginger, cranberry, puree, champagne, and schnapps into a metal shaker tin. Stir gently. Strain into champagne glass. Garnish with a raspberry. For an alcohol free version use a non-alcoholic champagne and substitute peach puree for the peach schnapps.

Barker demonstrates the proper technique for preparing lemon-twist garnishes.